SHONA

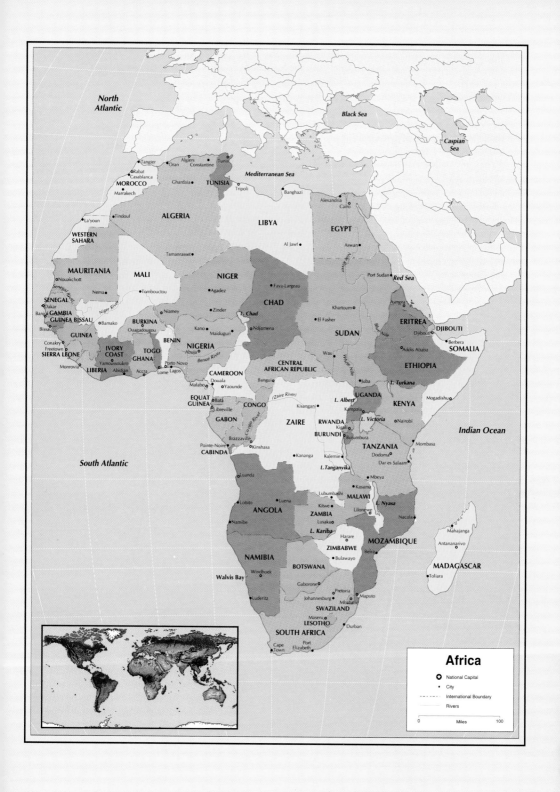

North
Atlantic

Black Sea

Caspian
Sea

Tangier
Algiers Constantine
Oran Tunis
Rabat
Casablanca
MOROCCO Ghardaia
Marrakech

Mediterranean Sea

TUNISIA
Tripoli
Banghazi

Alexandria
Cairo

La'youn Tindouf

WESTERN
SAHARA

ALGERIA

LIBYA

EGYPT

Aswan

Tamanrasset

Al Jawf

Port Sudan
Red Sea

MAURITANIA
Nouakchott

MALI

NIGER

Faya-Largeau

Asmera

CHAD
Nema

Tombouctou

Agadez

Khartoum

ERITREA

Senegal River

SENEGAL
Dakar

Niger River

Niamey

Zinder

L. Chad

El Fasher

Blue Nile

DJIBOUTI
Djibouti

Banjul
GAMBIA
GUINEA BISSAU
Bissau

Bamako

BURKINA
Ouagadougou

Kano
Maiduguri

Ndjamena

SUDAN

Berbera
SOMALIA

GUINEA
Conakry
Freetown
SIERRA LEONE
Monrovia

BENIN

IVORY
COAST
Yamoussoukro
LIBERIA Abidjan

TOGO
GHANA

Accra
Lome Lagos

NIGERIA
Abuja

Benue River

CAMEROON

Porto Novo

Douala
Malabo
Yaounde

Bangui

CENTRAL
AFRICAN REPUBLIC

Wau

White Nile

Juba

Addis Ababa

ETHIOPIA

L. Turkana

EQUAT.
GUINEA
Bata
Libreville

(Zaire River)

CONGO

GABON

Kisangani

L. Albert
UGANDA
Kampala

Mogadishu

KENYA

ZAIRE

RWANDA
Kigali
BURUNDI
Bujumbura

L. Victoria

Nairobi

Congo River

Brazzaville
Pointe-Noire
CABINDA

Kinshasa

Kananga

Kalemie

TANZANIA
Dodoma

Mombasa

Indian Ocean

South Atlantic

Luanda

L.Tanganyika

Dar es Salaam

Lubumbashi

Kasama

Mbeya

Lobito
Luena
ANGOLA
Namibe

Kitwe
ZAMBIA
Lusaka

MALAWI
Lilongwe

L. Nyasa

Nacala

L. Kariba
Harare

NAMIBIA
Windhoek

Walvis Bay

BOTSWANA

ZIMBABWE
Bulawayo

Belra

MOZAMBIQUE

Mahajanga

Antananarivo

MADAGASCAR
Toliara

Luderitz

Gaborone

Pretoria
Johannesburg Maputo
Mbabane
SWAZILAND

Maseru
LESOTHO

Durban

SOUTH AFRICA

Cape
Town
Port
Elizabeth

Africa

★ National Capital
• City
- - - International Boundary
— Rivers

0   Miles   100

The Heritage Library of African Peoples

SHONA

Gary N. van Wyk, Ph.D. and
Robert Johnson, Jr., J.D.

THE ROSEN PUBLISHING GROUP, INC.
NEW YORK

Published in 1997 by The Rosen Publishing Group, Inc.
29 East 21st Street, New York, NY 10010

First Edition

Manufactured in the United States of America

Library of Congress Cataloging-in-Publication Data

Van Wyk, Gary.
    Shona / Gary N. van Wyk and Robert Johnson, Jr. — 1st ed.
      p.   cm. — (The heritage library of African peoples)
    Includes bibliographical references and index.
    ISBN 0-8239-2011-9
    1. Shona (African people)—Juvenile literature. I. Johnson,
Robert, Jr., J.D. II. Title. III. Series.
DT2913.S55V36   1997
968.91′004963975—dc21   96-47359
                                      CIP
                                      AC

Contents

INTRODUCTION

THERE IS EVERY REASON FOR US TO KNOW something about Africa and to understand its past and the way of life of its peoples. Africa is a rich continent that has for centuries provided the world with art, culture, labor, wealth, and natural resources. It has vast mineral deposits, fossil fuels, and commercial crops.

But perhaps most important is the fact that fossil evidence indicates that human beings originated in Africa. The earliest traces of human beings and their tools are almost two million years old. Their descendants have migrated throughout the world. To be human is to be of African descent.

The experiences of the peoples who stayed in Africa are as rich and as diverse as of those who established themselves elsewhere. This series of books describes their environment, their modes of subsistence, their relationships, and their customs and beliefs. The books present the variety of languages, histories, cultures, and religions that are to be found on the African continent. They demonstrate the historical linkages between African peoples and the way contemporary Africa has been affected by European colonial rule.

Africa is large, complex, and diverse. It encompasses an area of more than 11,700,000 square miles. The United States, Europe, and India could fit easily into it. The sheer size is an indication of the continent's great variety in geography, terrain, climate, flora, fauna, peoples, languages, and cultures.

Much of contemporary Africa has been shaped by European colonial rule, industrialization, urbanization, and the demands of a world economic system. For more than seventy years, large regions of Africa were ruled by Great Britain, France, Belgium, Portugal, and Spain. African peoples from various ethnic, linguistic, and cultural backgrounds were brought together to form colonial states.

For decades Africans struggled to gain their independence. It was not until after World War II that the colonial territories became independent African states. Today, almost all of Africa is ruled by Africans. Large numbers of Africans live in modern cities. Rural Africa is also being transformed, and yet its people still engage in many of their customs and beliefs.

Contemporary circumstances and natural events have not always been kind to ordinary Africans. Today, however, new popular social movements and technological innovations pose great promise for future development.

George C. Bond, Ph.D., Director
Institute of African Studies
Columbia University, New York

Spirit mediums, such as the man seen here, are experts who communicate with the spirit world. A spirit possesses, or takes over, the medium's body and speaks through the medium. When possessed by the spirit of an ancestor, the medium is thought to actually become that person and speak to the living. In this way Shona ancestors can directly affect events in the world.

chapter

1

THE PEOPLE AND THE LAND

THE SHONA PEOPLE, NUMBERING ABOUT 7
million, live mostly in Zimbabwe. At different
times, Zimbabwe has been called Rhodesia
(1898–1953; 1965–1980), Southern Rhodesia
(1953–1965), and Zimbabwe-Rhodesia (1979–
1980). These name changes reflect the major
political changes that Shona territory has experi-
enced.

The Shona make up about 75 percent of
Zimbabwe's population. The second largest
group in Zimbabwe is the Ndebele (also called
the Matabele), who should not be confused
with the Ndebele who live in South Africa. The
Ndebele invaded Shona territory from what is
now South Africa around 1840. The tension
resulting from this invasion has affected the histories of these peoples.

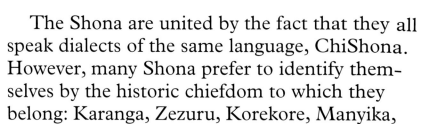

The Shona are united by the fact that they all speak dialects of the same language, ChiShona. However, many Shona prefer to identify themselves by the historic chiefdom to which they belong: Karanga, Zezuru, Korekore, Manyika, Ndau, or Kalanga.

The Shona are associated with two extraordinary phases of African history. First, they established a powerful trading empire that flourished for centuries. Second, the Shona have a long history of resistance to white colonial rule. White control began at the end of the 1800s. It ended only in 1980, when Rhodesia became the last British colony in Africa to become independent. At that time, it was renamed Zimbabwe.

Since about 900 AD, the mining and trading of precious metals in this region led to the rise of several powerful African states. Zimbabwe has many magnificent ruins of stone buildings, which were built when these states were powerful. The walls often have rows, or courses, of stone laid in decorative patterns. Ancient Shona artwork, including stone sculptures and gold objects from the 1400s, has been found among the buildings.

Shona people call these stone complexes *madzimbahwe*, (pronounced mud-zim-BAH-wee; the "*ma-*" in front of words indicates the plural in Shona). The largest and most impressive single *dzimbahwe* is called Great Zimbabwe. One of Africa's greatest built complexes, it is

Modern Zimbabwe is named after the ruins of stone settlements found throughout the country. *Dzimbahwe* means the court, home, or grave of a chief, and the Shona phrase *dzimba dza mabwe* means house of stone. The most famous *dzimbahwe* is Great Zimbabwe, seen here. This section of wall is over thirty feet high. The top is ornamented with a zigzag design and stone poles, called monoliths, which stick up into the sky.

so breathtaking that most European colonists refused to believe that it was built by Africans. Archaeology has since proven this fact. Because Great Zimbabwe is a powerful symbol of African achievement, when Rhodesia finally gained its freedom it adopted the new name Zimbabwe.

Shona religion shapes their society. For most Shona today the spiritual world of their ancestors is an ever-present fact. Even followers of Christian churches and sects among the Shona point out that the Bible encourages them to

11

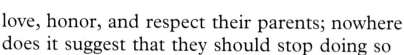

love, honor, and respect their parents; nowhere does it suggest that they should stop doing so once their parents are dead.

Religion played a key role in the Shona's two major wars against white rule. The First Chimurenga (war of liberation) was at the end of the 1800s; the Second Chimurenga was fought from 1966 to 1980. In both *chimurenga*s, the spirits of the Shona's ancestors urged their living relatives to fight. Their inspirational message was channelled through spirit mediums, holy people who have the power to communicate with the spirit world.

▼ THE LAND ▼

The Zimbabwean plateau has a pleasant climate and an elevation of over 3,000 feet above sea level. The plateau slopes gradually down to the Kalahari Desert in Botswana on the western side. On the other sides it drops down steeply toward the lowlands.

In the summer, these lowlands harbor health hazards such as malaria, spread by mosquitoes, and sleeping sickness, a disease carried by tsetse flies that is fatal to cattle. Tsetse flies attack in the hot, wet summer season from November to March. They pose no risk in the cold, dry period from April to October. This condition forced cattle herders to practice transhumance, the seasonal movement of the herds to make the most

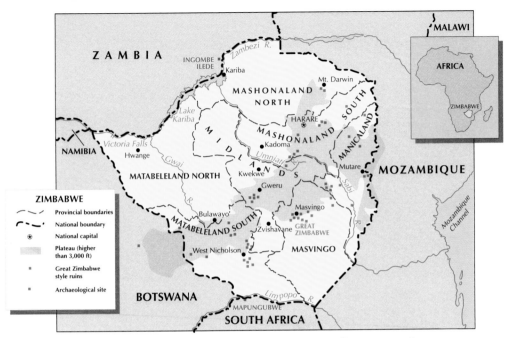

The geography of Zimbabwe has had a great influence on Shona history. The Zimbabwean plateau provided suitable conditions for herding, farming, and trade.

of the seasons and different environments. They moved their animals off the plateau in winter when the grass was dry, and took the herds to pasture in the moist lowlands while the tsetse threat was low there.

Farming on the plateau depends on the rains, which have never been dependable. This leads to periodic natural disasters that the Shona call *shangwa*. Every five years or so a drought occurs, which brings on other connected catastrophes, such as plagues of locusts. Farmers must have other sources of food or income to fall back on during years of *shangwa*.

Despite these drawbacks, the plateau is very pleasant, with plains of grassland and areas of

13

Soil and rainfall vary quite widely on the Zimbabwean plateau. The baobab trees seen here grow best in hot, dry regions.

woodland. The south and west areas are drier. Soil ranges from extremely fertile to very poor. Today, as in the past, farmers compete for the best soil and grazing lands. Numerous granite mountains rise above the plains, forming ridges of relatively smooth domes.

The plateau is rich in minerals and metals that occur in reefs close to the surface. Gold reefs lie inside extremely hard rocks, such as quartz. As rivers flow from the plateau down into the thickly wooded lowlands, they carve through the hard rock, washing out the gold inside. Today many Zimbabweans pan these rivers in the hope of finding gold. The Zimbabwean government tries to stop them and to control the mineral wealth of the plateau, which is probably what the rulers of Great Zimbabwe also did over 500 years ago.▲

chapter

2

RELIGION AND SOCIAL LIFE

SHONA TRADITIONS HAVE CHANGED A GREAT deal due to colonialism, the violent struggle against racial segregation, and the long war for independence. Nevertheless, aspects of Shona traditional culture still thrive in the rural areas of Zimbabwe and influence most Shona people's outlook on life.

▼ WORLDVIEW, PHILOSOPHY, ▼ AND RELIGION

The Supreme Being among the Shona is Mwari. Today Mwari is identified with the Christian God. However, before Christianity, Mwari was regarded as remote from the human world, too big and powerful to be concerned about people's everyday problems. Instead, Mwari appointed various spirits to act as mediators, or go-betweens. The kinds of spirits who

KINDS OF SPIRITS

1. *Vadzimu* is the group of ancestral spirits that continues to influence the lives of their living family members. The chief ancestral spirit, called the *mudzimu*, is usually that of the grandfather. Other important ancestral spirits are those of the mother and grandmother. Shona children are strictly taught to follow the ways of the ancestral spirits and to respect their elders. If a child shows disrespect toward or disobeys an elder, the elder's ancestral spirit may come back after death and cause problems for the child.

2. *Mhondoro* watches over the entire settlement and brings good things to the village. For example, if the rain is plentiful and the crops are abundant, people give thanks to the *mhondoro*. As a way of honoring the goodness of this spirit, a day of rest is observed in all villages.

3. *Nyanga* is a family of spirits that empowers Shona doctors, who also go by that name. These doctors diagnose and treat problems through divination, a process through which the spiritual causes of events and illnesses are uncovered. The doctors are believed to have descended from the earliest Shona doctors who were present when the community was founded.

4. *Shave* are the spirits of foreigners who die in Shona areas and are therefore not buried according to the customs of their own people. These spirits wander about constantly until they possess a medium. *Shave* spirits usually give special talents to their mediums, which the mediums use to benefit the community.

5. *Muroyi* are evil spirits. The person possessed by a *muroyi* is considered to be a witch, and when he or she dies, the evil spirit passes to his or her children.

have contact with Mwari are *vadzimu*, *mhondoro*, *nyanga*, *shave*, and *muroyi*.

Today, as in the past, ordinary people do not communicate directly with these spirits. They do so through the *masvikiro*, or spirit mediums. The *masvikiro* may be taken over or possessed by a spirit at any time, and the medium has no control over this occurrence. *Masvikiro* can try to invoke spirits, who may reveal themselves if they choose.

Music plays a vital role in contacting the spirits. Drums, *mbira* (thumb pianos), and other instruments are used. The music is played very fast. Some of the

The *mbira* (above) is a musical instrument played inside a hollow gourd (right). The metal keys of the *mbira* are mounted on a hollow wooden base, which serves as a sound box that enhances the sound. The musician's thumbs strike the keys, which can be tuned by adjusting their position under the metal bar that holds them in place.

audience members dance, while others clap. This activity calls forth the immortal spirits. Music and songs were sources of inspiration during both Shona wars of liberation.

Religion is closely related to medicine. If someone becomes ill, it might be the result of an offended spirit. Often sacrifices, such as slaughtering a goat, must be offered to the spirit to achieve a cure.

The spiritual world affects every aspect of daily life. Even Shona chiefs tend to be spiritual persons who claim their authority from their ancestors. When the community desires to appoint a chief, the *mhondoro* (community spirit) is consulted. A medium will then relay the spirit's choice. In essence, the chief is appointed by the *mhondoro*. The chief interprets and enforces customary law in the village. The land belongs to all the people and is a gift from the ancestors.

▼ SOCIAL LIFE AND CUSTOMS ▼

Shona culture is patrilineal, which means that descent and inheritance are traced through the male line. Each community has many extended families. To marry, a man must pay cattle to the father of the bride. Called a bride-price, this payment recognizes the cost and effort spent by the bride's parents on her upbringing. A man may marry as many women as he can support.

Many Shona continue to live in rural villages. Seen here is a family homestead in a rural area.

The community is run by a chief, who has a council of men to help him decide issues of law and custom.

The village tends to be a very tightly knit community, where a majority of the people are related. Each family has a main house where the husband and wife live together with their small children. Each family also has a granary, or *imba*. A typical village has a *dare*, or meeting place, where there are often large rocks on which men sit when they eat. About twenty to thirty yards from the main hut is the *danga*, an enclosed pen where cattle are kept at night. Periodically the Shona slaughter cattle for food or as sacrifices to the ancestors.

Harare, the capital of Zimbabwe, is a busy modern city. In the market, traders sell a wide variety of goods. The woman on the top left sells beads and baskets. The man (top right) holds traditional Shona knives; their sheaths are decorated with telephone wire. The men below (bottom left) make and sell items crafted from sheet metal. The street scene (bottom right) looks toward the Monomotapa Hotel, which is named after a Shona ruler who established relations with the Portuguese in the early 1500s.

The family unit is extremely tight. Each family member has specific duties. The grandfather on the father's side has the highest position in the family, followed by the father. The mother (the father's wife) has specific duties and has total control over her plot of land and the food for the family.

Men hunt and do the heavier physical tasks, while women cook and care for the homestead. Both sexes, however, help farm the land. The main food crops are corn, millet, rice, pumpkins, and sweet potatoes. The men and the boys take care of the cattle.

The wife's duties include looking after her husband and children and providing meals. She must also keep the homestead clean and tidy by sweeping and polishing the floors, usually once or twice a week. The wife gathers firewood for the fire in the house and grass for thatching the roof. She is also responsible for grinding or stamping the various cereals into meal, storing the crops, and fetching water for cooking and brewing beer.

These traditional duties have undergone considerable change as a result of increased education and exposure to new ideas. For example, in the cities of modern Zimbabwe, many women work outside the home, and both husband and wife share family responsibilities.▲

3

ART AND LITERATURE

THE SHONA HAVE RICH TRADITIONS OF ART and literature. The most famous art objects from Great Zimbabwe are pole-like sculptures with birds on the top. Carved from stone, these sculptures probably played an important religious role in early Shona society.

▼ SHONA STONE SCULPTURE ▼

Today modern Shona stone sculpture is world famous. This modern sculpture provides a cultural link with the ancient stone birds from the time of Great Zimbabwe.

Since the 1950s, many sculptors in Zimbabwe have begun to carve stone sculptures for sale to art lovers. These artworks quickly gained international popularity. They have been shown and bought by art museums all over the world.

Several different kinds of beautiful stone are

used, including soft soapstone; hard serpentine, quartz, and verdite; and spotted leopard stone. Colors are usually black or a shade of green, but pink, yellow, brown, and white stones are also used.

The sculptures both draw on themes from Shona religion and are influenced by the modern art of the West. Many sculptures show spirits turning into animals, or humans turning into spirits. Others are purely abstract in design, consisting only of interesting and pleasing shapes.

Although these works are generally called Shona sculpture, many of the artists come from neighboring countries. Stone sculpture has become a symbol of national pride in Zimbabwe. The National Gallery of Zimbabwe actively promotes the artists in many ways, as do several

Shona stone sculpture has become popular throughout the world. Sculptors often focus on traditional Shona themes, such as the drummer on the left, and create abstract human figures, such as the sculpture on top. The sculptures seen here were carved by Danai Nyadenga, a young Shona artist.

The rhinoceros is a popular subject for art. This three-foot-long wood carving was made near Great Zimbabwe for sale to tourists.

commercial galleries. Some sculptors have formed cooperatives, groups in which the members assist each other in producing and selling their work.

Some famous artists are Bernard Matemera, Nicholas Mukomberanwa, Henry Munyaradzi, Joseph Ndandarika, and Bernard and John Takawira.

Many other Zimbabweans make a living selling stone or wood carvings to tourists.

▼ TRADITIONAL ARTS ▼

Many ancient art forms are rarely made today. From very early times, Shona peoples made *bakatwa* (swords), spears, and *gano* (axes). The metal blades of these weapons have stamped patterns. Their wooden sheaths and handles are often decorated with very fine wire designs made from variously colored metals, which often included gold in the past.

Particularly beautiful are the very finely carved *mutsago* (wooden headrests), *tsvimbo* (short clubs), and staffs carved with human and animal figures. Many of these have been passed down from one generation to the next and are reminders of the ancestors who made and owned them. Some old axes, staffs, and *tsvimbo*

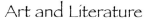

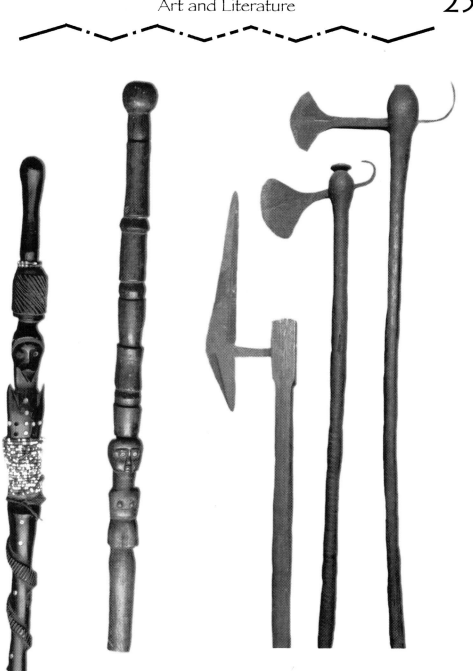

The staffs and axes seen here are examples of traditional Shona artwork. Staffs with human figures are used only by people who have high status or great spiritual power. Axes are important ceremonial objects, because to dance with an ax is to invite a spirit to possess you.

Ndoro shells (top right) were a form of currency before Europeans arrived. Europeans manufactured pottery and glass imitations of *ndoros* in different sizes, including beads in the shape of half-*ndoros* (far right and bottom right). Metal crosses (center) and cowrie shells (bottom left) were other forms of currency used for trade in this part of Africa. Much later, the British made coins for Rhodesia (top left), which had holes in the center like *ndoro* shells.

are still used during religious ceremonies to invite spirits to possess the user. New ones are also still made today.

Personal decoration was another important form of art. Chiefs and other high ranking people wore circular disks, which were made from the front end of shells found in the Indian Ocean. Called *ndoro*, these disks were one form of currency. *Ndoro* were also worn to invite spiritual possession. When the Portuguese learned of the value of *ndoro*, they mass-produced *ndoro* imitations for trade.

Other ancient art forms that are still continued today include weaving, bark cloth making, and basketry.

▼ SHONA LITERATURE ▼

Shona culture has a rich tradition of oral literature. Praise poetry celebrates the actions of ancient Shona heroes as well as contemporary political leaders. Folktales, proverbs, myths, legends, and a rich collection of songs all reflect the Shona worldview.

Contemporary Shona writers have creatively adapted themes and stylistic features of oral literature and songs to express more recent experiences in Zimbabwe.

The first generation of well-known Shona writers appeared before World War II, at a time when very few Africans had received Western education. Writers such as Stanlake Samkange, Lawrence Vambe, and Solomon Mutswairo focused on the problems of colonialism and racism. In their longing for independence and artistic freedom of expression, they recalled the past greatness of their people to provide inspirational role models in their work.

After World War II the white-controlled government intimidated intellectuals and writers who were demanding democracy for Zimbabwe.

One of the most notable and controversial writers during the 1970s was Dambudzo Marechera. He was expelled from the University of Zimbabwe for being involved in student uprisings. He then studied at the University of London's School of Oriental and African

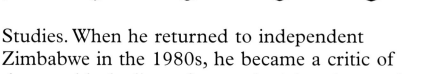

Studies. When he returned to independent Zimbabwe in the 1980s, he became a critic of the new black elites of postcolonial society and a champion of poor Zimbabwean farmers and workers.

More recent writers were still children during the war of liberation. Many of them have written about liberation and the problems and opportunities of the period after independence. The leading writers of this group include Chenjerai Hove, Tsitsi Dangeremba, and Chimmer Chinodya.

Zimbabwean writers provide unique commentaries on their society. Their writings have communicated Shona culture and politics to readers throughout the world.▲

chapter

4

EARLY HISTORY

THE EARLIEST BLACK PEOPLES TO SETTLE
on the Zimbabwean plateau may have arrived as
early as 200 AD. They were related to many
other African groups that are now found in
South Africa.

They settled in large villages close to rivers.
They farmed grain and herded sheep, goats, and
cattle. They also hunted and gathered wild
foods. Excavations near Great Zimbabwe at
Mabveni, the earliest village discovered south of
the Zambezi River, suggest that the people lived
in thatched houses with timber frameworks and
earthen walls, similar to rural architecture in
Zimbabwe today.

Trade linked settled groups whose different
environments offered contrasting advantages and
disadvantages. In the drier areas north and south

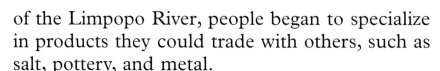

of the Limpopo River, people began to specialize in products they could trade with others, such as salt, pottery, and metal.

Before the end of the 900s, several small settlements on the Limpopo were involved in intercontinental trade with Arab and Muslim traders who visited the Indian Ocean coast. Africans traded gold, copper, iron, ivory, and leopard skins, and received in return Indian glass beads and imported fabric, among other items.

These small towns on the Limpopo, such as Mapungubwe, had stone architecture similar to later Shona towns. Among the archaeological finds at Mapungugwe was a beautiful sculpture of a rhinoceros covered in gold leaf.

Around 1000 AD the ancestors of the Shona arrived on the Zimbabwean plateau. They brought under their control those occupants already there and began the Shona-speaking chiefdoms that are still in place today. They placed great emphasis on cattle and were skilled in mining and using metal.

One group settled in the south where trade with the coast was already well established. They increased and controlled trade throughout the region. They grew so powerful that they dominated the plateau until around 1450. It was this group of Shona that built Great Zimbabwe.

▼ GREAT ZIMBABWE ▼

The highest part of Great Zimbabwe's impressive ruins is built on top of a natural granite dome. Erosion causes the granite rock to break off in layers. This "onion-peel weathering" results in heaps of broken slabs at the base of the domes.

The natural peeling process can be sped up by building fires on the rock and then chilling it with water. This causes the top layer of granite to crack off from the layer below like the shell of a boiled egg. Pieces broken off by this method can then be dressed, or trimmed, into slabs. This is how the rectangular slabs used to build Great Zimbabwe were made.

The thickness of the stone walls at Great Zimbabwe varies from four to seventeen feet; their height is about double their width. No mortar or other cementing material holds the rocks together; only the natural force of gravity. The walls taper from bottom to top; the thick bases carry the weight. The interiors of the walls are composed of rubble, but the outside faces are made of straight rows of carefully shaped stone. Sometimes the walls are decorated with rows of colored slabs. Ornamental patterns such as zigzags were formed by placing the rocks diagonally instead of flat.

The ruins are scattered over 100 acres, but the two main locations are the Hill Site and the Valley Site.

THE HILL SITE

Once called the Acropolis, the Hill Site can be reached by a step path. It leads up steep slopes that have been terraced with stone walls. The climb to the crest of the hill, crowned with towering walls, is both tiring and inspiring.

On top of the mountain, gray granite walls curve around and over rounded granite boulders. The shapes and the colors of the rocks blend with this natural environment. A series of terraced court-yards, some with raised platforms that probably once held sacred objects, are enclosed in this way. Visitors pass from one space to another through narrow passages and rounded doorways.

The top of the outer walls of the Hill Site has holes for stone pillars, or monoliths. A few mono-liths still stick up like horns from the walls. The Venda people of South Africa are related to the Shona and have similar symbols. These symbols convey the idea that the chief is like a bull who pro-tects his group.

Several soapstone monoliths sculpted in the form of birds have been found in the enclosures on the mountain. They were probably carved to honor the idea that birds are spiritual messengers between heaven and earth.

These stone birds are now in museums. Some are on display in the museum at the ruins. The Zimbabwe bird is the national symbol of present-day Zimbabwe and is displayed on the flag and on money.

From the Hill Site one can look down on the circular Great Enclosure in the Valley Site far below, as the tourist above is doing. The Hill Site is reached by a difficult climb up steep, step paths. The outer walls (below) are high and thick with very few entrance points.

In the past, the top of this wall would have had several monoliths and turrets. Both pictures show damaged sections of walls that were once very neatly built. Every stone in these buildings was shaped by hand.

THE VALLEY SITE

From the Hill Site the Valley Site can be seen far below. The Valley Site is dominated by the Great Enclosure, a set of massive stone walls that surround the place.

Inside the Great Enclosure are several smaller enclosures with stone walls. Within these relatively private spaces, several mud buildings once stood. Of course these mud structures have not survived.

One of the entrances into the Great Enclosure leads into the tall and narrow "parallel passage," or hallway. An interior wall was built to follow the curve of the outer wall.

The parallel passage leads directly to another impressive and puzzling feature: a pair of cone-shaped towers, one about thirty feet high, and the other much smaller. The large tower, tapering toward the top, is itself a wonder of African architecture. It shows the ancient architects' ability to create monumental forms of great sculptural beauty and power.

The outer wall reaches its highest point behind the tall tower and provides a dramatic backdrop. It is decorated with rows of stone laid in a zigzag pattern, and it once had monoliths standing along the top.

The two most famous and puzzling features of the Great Enclosure are the "parallel passage" (top) and the large cone-shaped tower (right). Nobody walking along the passage, which leads toward the tower, can be seen by anyone inside other parts of the complex. Both the tower and the passage show extremely fine techniques of building with stone.

INTERPRETING THE RUINS

Some experts believe that the Hill Site, perched on top of the mountain and reaching into the sky, was probably the most sacred part of the Shona settlement. Almost all of the Zimbabwe birds were discovered there. This is probably where the *masvikiro* lived and where important religious ceremonies took place. The hill's many enclosed courtyards of different sizes provide perfect spaces for both public and secret ceremonies.

While the ruler would have been required to participate in religious events on the hill, he probably lived in the Great Enclosure in the valley, close to the towers. The Great Enclosure was built at the height of the kingdom's power. The walls themselves, towering and enclosing, and the decorations on them reflected the power and status of the ruler. Once inside the Great Enclosure, the ruler would have been shielded from public view by the high outside walls. The Great Enclosure also had more private areas and hidden passages that the king could use without being observed by others inside the royal grounds.

Between the Great Enclosure and the Hill Site is a large open court, or *dare*. It is surrounded by the remains of several mud-brick houses connected by stone walls. Numerous houses without any grand enclosures, similar to those still in use in parts of Zimbabwe today, housed the ordinary people. Recent estimates suggest that Great Zimbabwe had 18,000 inhabitants.

To understand how the grand stone buildings of Great Zimbabwe were used and what they meant, we need to know how Zimbabwe society functioned.

▼ THE MEANING OF THE RUINS ▼

As in other African kingdoms, it is likely that Great Zimbabwe was the religious center of the region. In the view of most African religions, important people on earth become powerful ancestors after death. Thus great past leaders have a strong influence on the well-being of the state. They control life-and-death matters such as bringing forth or holding back the rain.

It is the duty of a living ruler to communicate with his powerful ancestors and keep them happy by performing sacrifices. In return, the ancestors ensure the well-being and fertility of the family, the cattle, and the crops. The ruler is a mediator who communicates messages between the ancestors of the chiefdom and his own people.

Two features of Great Zimbabwe appear to symbolize the religious role that the ruler played as a mediator. The cone-shaped towers in the Great Enclosure look like granaries, or storehouses for grain. Full granaries are the sign of fertile crops. The horn-shaped monoliths suggest that the chief is like a protective bull who looks after the people under him. In addition, it is the bull that fertilizes and increases the number of animals in the herd.

Taken together, these three ideas relating to crops, people, and the herd show the ruler's important duties in Shona society. However, the ruler can only perform properly by honoring his

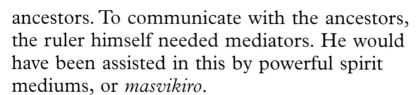

ancestors. To communicate with the ancestors, the ruler himself needed mediators. He would have been assisted in this by powerful spirit mediums, or *masvikiro*.

In Shona belief today, *masvikiro* are the specialists who communicate with the ancestors. Birds, particularly eagles, are also seen as messengers between humans and ancestors and between humans and the Supreme Being. In other words, birds are also mediators. If the early Shona had similar beliefs, then the Zimbabwe birds at Great Zimbabwe were probably powerful symbols of the *masvikiro*. They may have also referred to the ruler's own role as a mediator.

▼ THE TRADING STATE ▼

In the 500 years of Great Zimbabwe's influence, numerous changes must have occurred in the way the state operated and how it gained its wealth and power. Such changes are now very hard to chart.

Perhaps Great Zimbabwe first grew wealthy from its ideal location on the edge of the plateau. The early people may have practiced transhumance (the seasonal movement of grazing animals from mountain to lowland pastures). In this way the people were able to fatten their herds and hunt in the lowlands. The Great Zimbabwe region was good for farming. Local

INTERNATIONAL TRADE

Trade is based on the fact that buyers and sellers value items differently. For this reason, both Muslim traders and Africans were enthusiastic about the intercontinental trade that connected them from about 900 AD.

From India, traders brought cheaply produced glass beads and fabrics. For Africans, these items were very prestigious and were gladly exchanged for gold. Muslim traders saw gold as a form of currency and as a symbol of prestige. Africans, however, valued gold less than tougher and more practical metals such as iron and copper. Africans valued cattle above all and used them as currency. Cattle were vital both for marriage and for religious sacrifices that asked the ancestors to bring good rains and fertility to the land and the community.

Their Muslim trading partners saw things very differently. On the other side of the Indian Ocean, brides were required to wear ivory bangles. Swallowing crushed rhinoceros horn was believed to ensure human fertility . Perhaps this is what the gold rhinoceros of Mapungubwe symbolized: the power of the trade that stemmed from the fact that Africans and Muslims had such different values. The fact that gold and rhino horn were both vital to trade is the likely explanation for this sculpture.

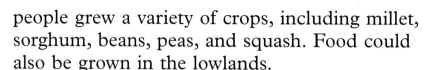

people grew a variety of crops, including millet, sorghum, beans, peas, and squash. Food could also be grown in the lowlands.

There was also plenty of timber and ore to smelt metals and forge useful tools, weapons, and ornaments. Other local industries probably included the weaving of textiles (begun earlier at Mapungubwe), and the making of graphite-polished pots, the remains of which have been found at Great Zimbabwe. This beautiful silvery pottery is still made there today.

Cattle have been and remain the single most important source of wealth for African herders. In Great Zimbabwe, a large, well-fattened herd was like a bank that could finance numerous other transactions; hunting products were simply a bonus. Cattle are also the basis of community life. It is through cattle, paid to a bride's family by the husband's family, that Shona families unite and grow.

Cattle also have great religious importance. Cattle must be sacrificed to bring harmony between people and their ancestors. The ancestors control the fortunes of human communities. Spiritual power is gained by sacrificing cattle, which are the basis of earthly power. On the other hand, earthly power implies spiritual power, since a person with many cattle is regarded as favored by the spirits. On the slopes of the hill at Great Zimbabwe, thousands of bone fragments, mostly from young cattle, have been found. It is likely that they were sacrificed for religious purposes and then eaten by the local elite.

This fortunate combination of factors and goods would have quickly made the early Great Zimbabwe a wealthy center for regional trade. It allowed the early kingdom to extend its trade links, wealth, and power across the plateau and beyond. Because the people considered wealth to be related to spiritual power, Great Zimbabwe was probably regarded with doubled awe by the surrounding people.

This rich trade probably caused Great Zimbabwe to change rapidly. Regional trade in practical items continued and may have even grown to include copper ingots from Ingombe Iledi, much farther inland. However, the import and export of prestige items became and remained the major focus.

In the period of greatest prosperity, stone complexes, called *madzimbahwe*, served as the regional capitals of chiefs who fell under the authority of the ruler of Great Zimbabwe, the main capital.

Most of the plateau's population lived in rural villages, far away from the *madzimbahwe*. These rural people were involved with farming and herding in the summer. In the winter they con-

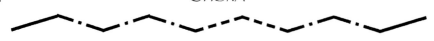

centrated on hunting and mining. They delivered
the gold, ivory, rhinoceros horns, pelts, and
other luxury items to the elite class at the
various *madzimbahwe*. In this way, precious
resources flowed into the regional capitals. They
were then transported onward to Great
Zimbabwe from which they were redistributed
through trade. The elites may also have required
the rural people to support them by providing
the cattle and crops consumed within the
madzimbahwe.

The elites of the many *madzimbahwe* lived in
walled enclosures, separated from the ordinary
people. Despite the value of cattle as currency,
or perhaps as a show of wealth, the elite ate
mostly beef. The poorer people ate sheep, goats,
and wild animals.

It is hard to understand why the rural people
tolerated this situation. Respect for, and even
fear of, the capital may have been a factor. To
ensure the continued loyalty of the people, the
elites may have rewarded them with some valu-
able items. Cattle would have been most appre-
ciated, followed by useful items such as iron
tools, pottery, salt, and cloth. Fancy ornaments
would have been inappropriate for ordinary
people and would have been useless if a disas-
trous *shangwa* arrived and the people had little
to eat.

Finds at Great Zimbabwe include Chinese

pottery from the Ming Dynasty (1368–1644), glazed stoneware from Iran, and Islamic glass made during the 1200s and 1300s.

Great Zimbabwe was a capital of great luxury and status. Many experts believe that the architecture's main function was to impress all who saw it with the power of the state. Like the pyramids of Egypt, visitors to Great Zimbabwe today are amazed by the amount of labor that the state controlled in order to build the complex.

But if Great Zimbabwe had become overly obsessed with its symbols of power and status and lost sight of the practical needs of life and the realities of its people, its survival would have become threatened. It is also in such situations that Shona chiefs today lose the human support and spiritual backing that are seen as essential for their authority.

▼ THE DECLINE OF GREAT ZIMBABWE ▼

By 1450 Great Zimbabwe had declined. Perhaps it had grown too large and used up too many of the surrounding natural resources, such as grassland, timber, and ore, to survive. Perhaps a *shangwa* arrived in the form of a devastating drought that killed crops and cattle. The failure of the rains would have suggested a serious spiritual failure on the part of the ruler and his ancestors. This may have further upset the surrounding population, who appear to have been

There is a great contrast between the grandeur of Great Zimbabwe (top) and the way that ordinary villagers lived in the past and continue to live today (bottom). One theory about the decline of Great Zimbabwe is that its rulers lost touch with the needs of ordinary people.

forced to contribute more to the capital than they received in return. Perhaps the king's *masvikiro* deserted him.

In any event, groups began to break away from Great Zimbabwe's control and establish their own states based on its pattern. Through these breakaway groups, Zimbabwe culture continued in different ways for several centuries. One important breakaway group, called the Mwenemutapa state, survived until 1917.

Another important breakaway group, called the Rozvi, established a trading state that survived until it was defeated by the Ndebele invaders in the early 1800s.▲

chapter

5

COLONIAL RULE AND INDEPENDENCE

IN 1839 THE NDEBELE, LED BY MZILIKAZI, settled at Bulawayo. From that time on, the presence of the Ndebele had a great influence on the Shona and the history of the country that later became known as Zimbabwe. The territory under Mzilikazi's control became known as Matabeleland. The Ndebele king was recognized as overlord by the local Kalanga Shona chiefs, but never by the Shona chiefs farther away in Mashonaland. The Kalanga were incorporated as the lowest class of Ndebele society.

▼ KING LOBENGULA AND ▼ CECIL RHODES

In 1870 Mzilikazi's son Lobengula inherited his father's throne. At that time, the British and the Afrikaner Boers, settlers of Dutch background, were competing for control in southern Africa. Their firearms gave them great power over kingdoms such as the Ndebele.

The Boers controlled the rich gold mines of South Africa. Cecil John Rhodes was an English millionaire who had grown rich from mining (mainly diamonds) in South Africa. He planned to seize control of the gold mines of Mashonaland for Britain. He would justify this by claiming that Lobengula, the Ndebele leader, controlled all the Shona and had permitted the British takeover. In fact, Lobengula had no authority over most of Mashonaland.

In 1888 Lobengula, who could not read, was tricked into signing a written treaty that gave the British unlimited freedom to start mines in the kingdom. The treaty left out the key items that were the basis of Lobengula's verbal consent. During discussions he had made it clear that he would retain authority as king.

Rhodes's agents falsely informed the British government that Lobengula had given them the right to occupy Mashonaland. Queen Victoria allowed Rhodes to start a private company, called the British South Africa Company (BSAC), to control Mashonaland, although Lobengula wrote to tell her he had been tricked.

In 1890 Rhodes sent a group of settlers to Mashonaland, where they built several forts,

The famous landmark Victoria Falls (above), located on the Zambezi River, was named after Queen Victoria by the missionary David Livingstone in 1855. Local people know the falls as Mosi-oa-Tunya, which means the smoke that thunders, referring to the clouds of spray that can be seen for many miles around.

including Fort Victoria (now called Masvingo) and Fort Salisbury (now Harare).

▼ BRITISH OCCUPATION ▼

In Mashonaland the BSAC allowed settlers to take land that belonged to the natives and treat them brutally. Chiefs were forced to provide laborers, who had to work for a month without pay. Then the British imposed a "hut tax" on every dwelling. The Shona had to sell their possessions or work for settlers in order to get cash, which they had never used before.

The Shona blamed Lobengula for the British occupation. They refused to pay their annual taxes and raided Ndebele cattle. The Ndebele

48

launched a minor attack on the Shona near
Fort Victoria in 1893. Mgandani, the Ndebele
general who led the battle, was captured by the
British and mutilated. This provoked the Anglo-
Ndebele War.

The British had failed to discover profitable
gold fields in Mashonaland. The war gave the
British the excuse they needed to destroy
Ndebele power and take over Ndebele land and
cattle, thus reducing their losses. Lobengula had
hoped to avoid armed conflict with the British,
but now he was forced to fight them. He was
defeated at two major battles. To avoid capture,
Lobengula retreated north after burning his capital. In 1894 he died at a place north of the
Zambezi River.

The British quickly divided Matabeleland
among themselves. Each of
the 948 settlers received
approximately 6,350
acres. Favoritism
allowed some set-
tlers, such as Sir John
Willoughby, to receive as

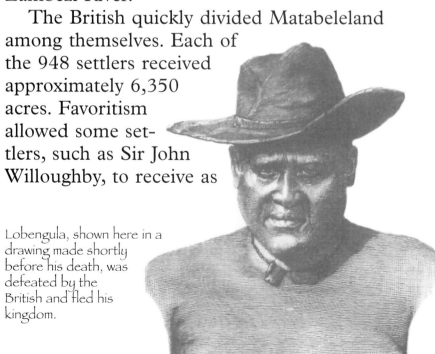

Lobengula, shown here in a
drawing made shortly
before his death, was
defeated by the
British and fled his
kingdom.

much as 600,000 acres. The Africans were forced to live on reserves where they had to pay monthly rents to foreign settlers living on their ancestral lands. By 1895 the Ndebele were left with only about 75,000 of their cattle, once estimated to number between 200,000 and 300,000.

Cecil Rhodes now claimed the whole of Zimbabwe. In 1895 he named the country Rhodesia after himself.

▼ REBELLION ▼

In March 1896 the Ndebele struck back against the settlers. In one week 122 men and eight settler women and children were killed. A few months later, the Shona chiefs rose up in a united rebellion. In this revolt, known as the First Chimurenga, 372 settlers were killed. Punishing attacks were launched against the African population: 8,000 were killed.

Spirit mediums played a key role in the First Chimurenga. They channeled messages from the most sacred royal ancestors of the Shona and from Mwari, the Supreme Being, who urged the Shona to get rid of the European invaders. One of the most important ancestral spirits, or *mhondoro*, was Nehanda, the female founder of the Shona nation. Her influence was felt over many chiefdoms, and this helped to coordinate resistance.

A woman called Charwe was a medium for the *mhondoro* spirit Nehanda. Charwe was captured in 1897, after the leading Shona chiefs had been executed or defeated. Sentenced to death, she refused to convert to Christianity and remained defiant even as she was about to be hanged. She predicted that her "bones would rise" to defeat the whites.

▼ RHODESIA: A BRITISH COLONY ▼

In 1914 the rule of Rhodes's BSAC ended. Britain took direct control and formed the colony of Southern Rhodesia in 1923. Only whites who owned property and earned over a certain income had the right to vote.

Southern Rhodesia passed laws to separate the races; deprived blacks of political, economic, and social rights; and forced blacks off their ancestral lands. Blacks were paid one-tenth of what whites received for the same job, and they received very little education.

Shona and Ndebele leaders realized that they should unify against white rule. Their cooperation gave birth to what is known as Zimbabwe African nationalism. In 1932 the African National Congress (ANC) of Southern Rhodesia was started by Aaron Jacha, a Shona.

In the decades that followed, moderate black leaders worked within the colonial system trying to soften laws that discriminated against blacks.

Hard-line leaders said this was not enough. They demanded the complete overthrow of colonial rule and the establishment of a true democracy through majority rule.

When the white government banned African political parties, moderate black leaders started new parties. After the ANC was banned, Joshua Nkomo, a Kalanga who continues to play a role in Zimbabwean politics today, formed the Zimbabwe African People's Union (ZAPU). A more hard-line party called the Zimbabwe African National Union (ZANU) was formed by exiled nationalists in Tanzania. The ZANU leader Robert Mugabe is currently prime minister and effective leader of Zimbabwe.

The Rhodesian government tried to inflame ethnic tension between the Ndebele-dominated ZAPU and the Shona-dominated ZANU. In reality, both parties contained members of both ethnic groups, but there were tensions between them.

▼ INTERNATIONAL SUPPORT ▼

African nationalists pressured Britain to halt the repression and violation of human rights in its colony of Southern Rhodesia. But this only made Southern Rhodesia more defiant of world opinion; it decided to declare itself independent of Britain.

Renamed Rhodesia, it was led by Ian Smith. Rhodesia became a rebel colony that was cut off

In both the First and the Second Chimurenga (war of liberation), Shona soldiers were inspired by the spirit of Nehanda, the first female ancestor of the nation. Nehanda's spirit spoke through a medium named Charwe. When Zimbabwe became free in 1980, special cloths were printed to celebrate the victory and honor Nehanda. On the skirt of the woman seen here, Charwe appears at the top with Robert Mugabe, the first prime minister of Zimbabwe, below.

from most of the world. Economic sanctions were declared against them, meaning that most countries would not trade with them. To those who asked if Rhodesia would ever be ruled by the black majority, Smith declared, "Not in a thousand years."

▼ THE SECOND CHIMURENGA ▼

The Second Chimurenga, or war of liberation, began when African nationalists announced that they would win their freedom by armed struggle. While Joshua Nkomo was imprisoned in 1964, ZAPU was led by James Chikerema, a Shona. ZAPU continued to use diplomacy to try to improve the situation. Meanwhile ZANU dedicated itself to a socialist revolution that would eliminate private ownership of land and minerals.

The Smith government used powerful propaganda to make whites hate the black nationalists. Although some whites saw through the propaganda and assisted the liberation movements, most believed the government's misinformation and became more racist. The Smith regime also tried to promote ethnic tensions among blacks and to convince them that the freedom fighters were "terrorists" who would introduce communism and take their children away from them.

However, ZANU and ZAPU got their message across to the people. For example, ZANU forces

This painting shows the admiration that rural people felt for the guerrillas. Young school children often assisted the guerrillas. A photograph taken during the Second Chimurenga inspired this painting.

held secret meetings at night called *pungwes,* in the bush to educate rural villagers about the freedom struggle. They made radio broadcasts from neighboring countries and gave out pamphlets. Freedom songs and *pungwes* expressed the idea that the spirits of the great Shona ancestors, such as Nehanda, supported the struggle. Rural people fondly called the guerrillas *vakhomana,* meaning the boys. They provided food, clothes, and other aid to the guerrillas. Young schoolchildren served a vital role as *mujibas,* gatherers of information and messengers. They reported everything that was going on in the countryside.

To eliminate this kind of cooperation between the guerrillas and the people, the Rhodesian government forced almost 750,000 rural people into "protected villages" that were like concentration camps. Many lived under curfew from dusk till noon. Other villages were brutally intimidated; thousands were tortured and murdered. All of this only increased the people's commitment to the freedom struggle.

In 1979, when the war finally ended, 370 white and 10,000 black fighters had been killed in action (according to the Rhodesian government). Guerrilla attacks and land mine explosions had killed 378 white civilians; thousands of black civilians had been killed by the Rhodesians.

▼ BISHOP MUZOREWA ▼

The Rhodesian regime found another way to divide black opinion. They set up Bishop Abel Muzorewa as a puppet African leader who was against the socialist policies of ZANU and ZAPU. A puppet leader is someone whose acts are controlled by an outside influence. In 1979 the regime staged a false election that excluded ZANU and ZAPU and installed Bishop Muzorewa as prime minister of the country, renamed Zimbabwe-Rhodesia.

Britain, then under the conservative government led by Margaret Thatcher, was pressured by world opinion to organize a free and fair election that included ZANU and ZAPU. On

December 21, 1979, a cease-fire was declared
after Robert Mugabe and Joshua Nkomo agreed
to British-supervised elections. Britain was eager
to solve the problem of Rhodesia through an
election. However, like the Rhodesians, Britain
hoped that Robert Mugabe would not come to
power because Thatcher's government was
against socialism.

▼ PEACE AND INDEPENDENCE ▼

The British delayed Mugabe's return from
exile to Zimbabwe for a month after the cease-
fire. Mugabe's welcome-home rally drew the
largest crowd ever seen in Zimbabwe. The
British and Rhodesian governments were
alarmed at Mugabe's support because it
showed he might win the election. There were
assassination attempts on his life and a smear
campaign that included tactics such as blowing
up churches and blaming it on Mugabe
supporters.

Mugabe was forced to keep a very low profile,
while the Rhodesians supported Muzorewa's
expensive, high-profile election campaign. When
the election results were announced on March
4, 1980, Mugabe had won by a huge majority,
as most Zimbabweans expected. He had fifty-
seven seats against Nkomo's twenty. Muzorewa
only won three. Rhodesian whites who had
believed Smith's propaganda were shocked at

Rhodesia was the last British colony in Africa to become independent. South Africa, which ceased to be a British colony in 1961, remained under white rule until 1994. The struggle for democracy in both these countries received wide international support. Seen above is an Independence Day celebration in a stadium in Harare.

the results. Thousands fled to South Africa, which was still under white rule at that time.

At the Independence Day celebrations, the famous reggae star Bob Marley played songs dedicated to the Zimbabwean struggle. Zimbabwean pop songs thanked the ancestors for their support. A special cloth was printed with a picture of Mugabe, now prime minister, under the guiding spirit of Nehanda's medium, Charwe. The statue of Cecil Rhodes in the heart of downtown Harare was pulled down. Rhodesia had finally become Zimbabwe.

Mugabe's government urged national reconciliation and included both Ndebele and white

Robert Mugabe's government promoted reconciliation between the races in many ways. White politicians were included in government, and many whites were allowed to keep their positions in the military. Seen here is the first president of Zimbabwe, Rev. Canaan Banana, reviewing troops. His duties as president were mainly ceremonial.

politicians. Unfortunately, political and ethnic rivalries between Shona and Ndebele led to violent repression in Matabeleland. But after several years, Mugabe and Nkomo reached a new

One of the main aims of the liberation struggle in Zimbabwe was to return land to black ownership. Today much of the land and the economic power of Zimbabwe are still controlled by whites. Many Shona, such as this woman picking tobacco, continue to work as laborers on white-owned farms.

agreement and Zimbabweans began to experience true peace. Many reforms have been introduced to bring about a fairer society, but much economic power remains in the hands of whites.

The new government has discouraged political opposition, and many believe this condition does not promote freedom and democracy. However, the majority of Shona people continue to reelect Robert Mugabe and his party.

The Shona today are not only proud of their great history, they are also in control of present-day events in Zimbabwe. Many Shona leaders are dedicated to improving the future of Zimbabwe for all its peoples.▲

Glossary

Afrikaner An Afrikaans-speaking South African of Dutch descent.

ancestor worship Belief that the spirits of ancestors have power over the living.

chimurenga War of liberation.

danga Cattle-holding area.

dare Meeting place.

elite Group privileged because of its wealth, education, or power.

imba Granary.

ingots Metal that has been molded into a standardized shape and weight.

masvikiro Spirit mediums.

propaganda Information, ideas, or rumors that are spread to damage or aid a political cause.

pungwe Meeting held in the bush by guerrillas.

sanctions Economic punishment against countries that break international law.

shangwa Disaster.

spirit medium Religious person who channels messages from ancestral spirits.

transhumance Seasonal and alternating movement of herds.

61

For Further Reading

Ellert, H. *The Material Culture of Zimbabwe.*
Harare, Zimbabwe: Longman, 1984.
Frederikse, Julie. *None But Ourselves: Masses vs.
Media in the Making of Zimbabwe.*
Johannesburg: Ravan Press, 1982.
Mor, F. *Shona Sculpture.* Harare, Zimbabwe:
Jongwe, 1987.

Challenging Reading

Bourdillon, Michael. *The Shona Peoples.* Gweru,
Zimbabwe: Mambo Press, 1991.
Hall, Martin. *The Changing Past: Farmers, Kings
and Traders in Southern Africa, 200–1860.* Cape
Town: David Philip, 1987.
Lan, David. *Guns and Rain: Guerrillas and Spirit
Mediums in Zimbabwe.* Berkeley, CA: University of California Press, 1990.
Mugabe, Robert G. *Our War of Liberation.*
Gweru, Zimbabwe: Mambo Press, 1983.

Index

ABOUT THE AUTHORS

Gary van Wyk, a Zimbabwean, holds graduate degrees in law and fine arts, and a Ph.D. in Art History and Archaeology from Columbia University, New York. Currently Editor of Special Projects at The Rosen Publishing Group, he is engaged in a range of educational, scholarly, and museum projects on African culture. He recently spoke on Great Zimbabwe at a symposium on African cities held jointly by the Museum for African Art and the Guggenheim Museum in New York.

Robert Johnson Jr., currently Assistant Professor in the Dept. of Africana Studies at the University of Massachusetts, has also taught African history at Ithaca College and Brandeis University. With a background in government, he obtained both a Master's in African and African American Studies and a Doctor of Law degree from Cornell University. He has lived both in west and in east Africa, where his play *Mama's Boy* premiered at the Kenya National Theatre in 1972. His forthcoming book is entitled *Law and the Public Policy of Race*.

PHOTO CREDITS

Cover, pp. 8, 11, 17 (bottom), 19, 20 (all), 35 (bottom), 44 (top and bottom), 58 © William J. Dewey; pp. 14, 60 © Eric. L. Wheater; pp. 17 (top), 24, 25, 26 by Ira Fox, courtesy of G. van Wyk; p. 23 (top and bottom) courtesy of G. van Wyk; p. 33 (top and bottom) by Herbert W. Booth III © Gamma Liaison International; p. 35 (top) by Wendy Stone © Gamma Liaison International; pp. 48, 59 by J. Hahn © Maryknoll Missioners; p. 49 courtesy of the South African Library, Cape Town; p. 53 by J. McLaughlin © Maryknoll Missioners; p. 55 © Gary van Wyk.

CONSULTING EDITOR AND LAYOUT
Gary van Wyk, Ph.D.

SERIES DESIGN
Kim Sonsky

FOR FURTHER RESEARCH

BOOKS

Kari A. Cornell, *E-Cigarettes and Their Dangers*. San Diego, CA: ReferencePoint Press, 2020.

Erin Pack and Philip Wolny, *Everything You Need to Know About Alcoholism*. New York: Rosen Publishing, 2020.

Jennifer Peters, *Alcohol Abuse*. New York: Rosen Publishing, 2019.

David Sheff and Nic Sheff, *High: Everything You Want to Know About Drugs, Alcohol, and Addiction*. Boston, MA: Houghton Mifflin Harcourt, 2019.

INTERNET SOURCES

"Alcohol and Drug Abuse Statistics," *American Addiction Centers*, February 3, 2020. www.americanaddictioncenters.org.

"Guide for Children of Addicted Parents," *American Addiction Centers*, September 30, 2019. www.americanaddictioncenters.org.

"Opioid Overdose Crisis," *National Institute on Drug Abuse*, February 2020. www.drugabuse.gov.